# Charlotte's Web

by
E. B. White

## Teacher Guide
Written by
Anne Troy

> **Note**
> The Harper Trophy paperback edition of the book was used to prepare this guide. The page references may differ in the hardcover or other paperback editions.
>
> **Please note:** Please assess the appropriateness of this book for the age level and maturity of your students prior to reading and discussing it with your class.

**ISBN 1-56137-026-6**
Copyright infringement is a violation of Federal Law.

© 2000, 2004 by Novel Units, Inc., Bulverde, Texas. All rights reserved. No part of this publication may be reproduced, translated, stored in a retrieval system, or transmitted in any way or by any means (electronic, mechanical, photocopying, recording, or otherwise) without prior written permission from Novel Units, Inc.

Photocopying of student worksheets by a classroom teacher at a non-profit school who has purchased this publication for his/her own class is permissible. Reproduction of any part of this publication for an entire school or for a school system, by for-profit institutions and tutoring centers, or for commercial sale is strictly prohibited.

Novel Units is a registered trademark of Novel Units, Inc.

Printed in the United States of America.

To order, contact your local school supply store, or—

Novel Units, Inc.
P.O. Box 433
Bulverde, TX 78163-0433

Web site: www.educyberstor.com

# Table of Contents

**Summary** .................................................. 3

**Initiating Activities** ................................... 3

**Twenty-Two Chapters** ............................... 12
   Chapters contain: Vocabulary Words and
   Activities, Discussion Questions and Activities,
   Supplementary Activities, Predictions

**Post-reading Questions** ............................. 40

**Culminating Activities** .............................. 41

**Teacher Facts about Spiders** ..................... 41

**Using the *Charlotte's Web* Poster** ............ 43

**Assessment for *Charlotte's Web*** .............. 44

# Skills and Strategies

**Thinking**
Brainstorming, classifying and categorizing, evaluating, analyzing details, visualizing, synthesizing ideas, K-W-L strategy, comparing and contrasting

**Literary Elements**
Character, setting, plot development, story map, conflict, theme, suspense, imagery

**Vocabulary**
Synonyms/antonyms, classification

**Comprehension**
Predicting, sequencing, cause/effect, inference, make judgements, compare information from more than one source

**Writing**
Narrative, expository

**Listening/Speaking**
Participation in discussion and cooperative groups, entertain others with dramatic activities

## Summary
Wilbur, a weak baby pig, becomes Fern's pet. Wilbur is saved from certain death by his clever friend, Charlotte, the spider. Wilbur wins a prize at the fair and his life is saved but poor Charlotte lays her eggs at the fair and dies. She leaves behind an egg sac of spider children which Wilbur brings back to the farm so that he may watch over them until they hatch and reach maturity.

## Initiating Activities
1. Look at the cover of this novel. What is unusual about the illustration? *(The girl is carrying a real pig.)* Can you find any clues about the story? the characters?

2. There are several types of stories: realistic, biographical, historical and fantasy. Do you know what each of these types is? Can you name books that might fit in each of these categories? (Teacher writes class responses on a large piece of paper or the board.)

3. What type of story do you think this will be?

4. Many stories have the same parts—a setting, a problem, a goal, and a series of events that lead to an ending or a conclusion. These story elements may be placed on a story map. Just as a road map helps a driver get from one place to another, so too a story map helps the reader to understand the direction of the story. There are many different types of story maps. Students may use the one included or make up their own. (See page 4 of this guide.)

   We need answers to some questions which we'll look for as we begin the novel:

   — Who is the main character?
   — Where does the story take place?
   — What is the problem?

© Novel Units, Inc.                                                    All rights reserved

## Story Map

Characters _____

_____

Time and Place _____

_____

Problem _____

_____

_____

Goal _____

_____

_____

Beginning ⟶ Development ⟶ Outcome

_____

_____

_____

_____

_____

Resolution _____

_____

_____

_____

© Novel Units, Inc.   All rights reserved

As the story is read, more characters may be added, and the setting and problem may change. After each chapter is read, changes should be made.

5. Prereading Discussion Questions on Themes in the Story:

   Independence: What do you like about growing up? What don't you like about it? When do you like to be on your own? When do you like to have help?

   Selfishness: With whom do you have to share things? When do you think a kid *should* be expected to share? When do you think a kid should have the choice *not* to share? Do you think your parents are fair about what they expect you to share? What does it mean to be "selfish"? Are you ever selfish?

   Pets: Have you ever had a pet? What are the responsibilities as far as taking care of the pet? What happens if you do not care for your pet?

   Running Away: Have you ever run away or thought about it? If so, why? What happened? What other solution could you have tried first?

   Loneliness: Prereading Mapping of Theme (bulletin board idea) — Write the word "loneliness" in capital letters in the center of a large piece of paper. Have the students free associate (tell whatever ideas come to mind when they hear the word "loneliness"). Jot down students' ideas around the central word, helping students organize their ideas by category. A sample map outline with some sample ideas appears on page 7.

6. Role-play the following situations:

   — A mother tells a son that he should share a prized possession.

   — You are at camp for the first time and you feel miserable.

7. Bulletin Board: Make a large web using acrylic polymer or other materials available at Halloween, or draw the web on a large sheet of paper with black marker. The new vocabulary words for each chapter may be placed on the web. The class predictions may be posted below or beside the web.

# Charlotte's Web

**Recommended Procedure**
This book may be used in several ways: a) read to the entire class; b) read with the class; c) read in reading groups; d) read by an individual.

This book may be read one chapter at a time using the DRTA, Directed Reading Thinking Activity, Method. This technique involves reading a section, and then predicting what will happen next by making good guesses based on what has already occurred in the story. The predictions are recorded, and verified after the subsequent reading has taken place. (See pages 10-11 of this guide.)

The Discussion Questions and Activities at the end of each chapter, as well as any Supplementary Activities are provided so that you may, using discretion, make selections from them that will be suitable for use by the children in your group.

You may wish to have students show knowledge of words in the vocabulary before reading the chapter by writing simple definitions in their own words. After reading, the students may need to redefine the words by referring to the text and/or a dictionary.

## Sample Map Outline

**Synonyms**

1. Sadness from lack of companions or sympathy

2. Depression because of being alone

**Being the new kid at school**

1. No one to eat with

2. _____

3. _____

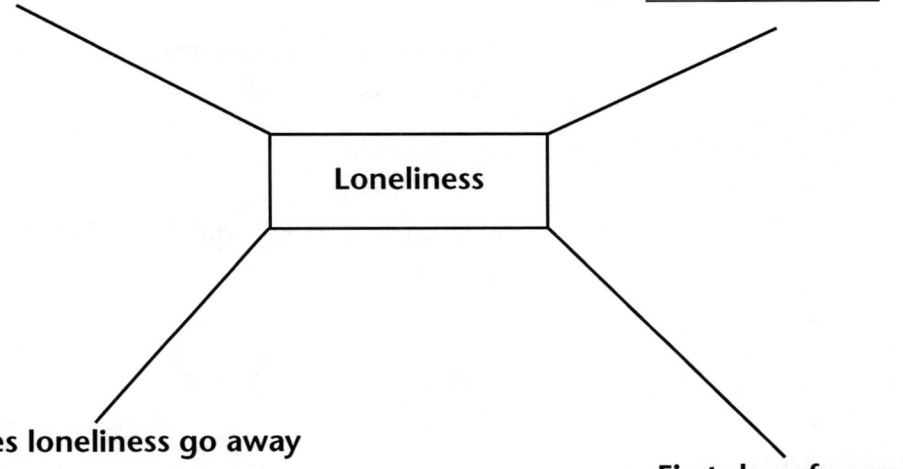

Loneliness

**What makes loneliness go away**

1. Phoning a friend

2. _____

3. _____

**First day of camp**

1. Missing my dog

2. _____

3. _____

© Novel Units, Inc.  All rights reserved

## Anticipation Guide

**Directions:** Read each of the following statements and label each "A" for "Agree" or "D" for "Disagree." See if any of your attitudes change after reading the story.

**Before Reading**     **After Reading**

_____         _____         Running away never solves anything.

_____         _____         If I had to choose between freedom and safety, I would choose safety.

_____         _____         Wild animals don't make good pets.

_____         _____         Animals can't really talk.

_____         _____         It is good to share.

## Graphic Organizers

Included in this guide are several types of graphic organizers, such as the Venn diagram, the T-Diagram, and brainstorming or cluster circles. A variety of possible answers should be listed by the teacher either on large sheets of paper or the chalkboard. Only then should the students be asked to develop their own graphics. Students are encouraged to express their opinions, and to state what they know about a topic. The teacher lists these opinions and "facts" and later, as the children read and discover that some of their ideas are incorrect, these ideas may be crossed out on the sheets or board. Students should be encouraged to elaborate on their answers, justify their opinions, prove their predictions, and relate what they have read to their own lives.

T-diagrams show likenesses and differences of two characters, plots, settings, etc.

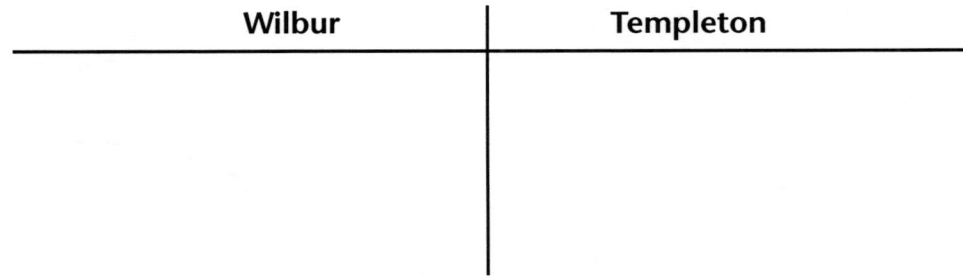

Venn diagrams are taken from math. Characteristics of two characters are listed, and the overlap or similarity may be seen.

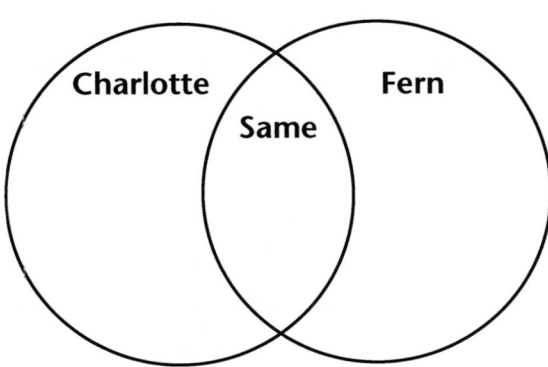

## Using Predictions

We all make predictions as we read—little guesses about what will happen next, how the conflict will be resolved, which details given by the author will be important to the plot, which details will help to fill in our sense of a character. Students should be encouraged to predict, to make sensible guesses. As students work on predictions, these discussion questions can be used to guide them: What are some of the ways to predict? What is the process of a sophisticated reader's thinking and predicting? What clues does an author give us to help us in making our predictions? Why are some predictions more likely than others?

A predicting chart is for students to record their predictions. As each subsequent chapter is discussed, you can review and correct previous predictions. This procedure serves to focus on predictions and to review the stories.

- Use the facts and ideas the author gives.
- Use your own knowledge.
- Use new information that may cause you to change your mind.

Predictions:
_____
_____
_____
_____

## Prediction Chart

| What characters have we met so far? | What is the conflict in the story? | What are your predictions? | Why did you make those predictions? |
|---|---|---|---|
|  |  |  |  |

## Chapter I: "Before Breakfast" — Pages 1-7

**Vocabulary**

| | | | |
|---|---|---|---|
| runt 1 | litter 3 | weakling 3 | injustice 3 |
| untimely 4 | specimen 5 | distribute 5 | promptly 5 |
| blissful 7 | | | |

**Vocabulary Activity**
List the vocabulary words on the board or on a sheet of paper in the form of a table. Pronounce the words. Ask the students to rate their knowledge of each of the words as a group or individually.

| Word | I Can Define | I Have Heard | I Don't Know |
|---|---|---|---|

**Discussion Questions and Activities**
1. Mr. Arable was going to do away with the runt pig. What does "do away with" mean? *(to kill)*

2. How did Fern stop her father from killing the baby pig? *(Page 3, She asked her father if she had been small at birth if he would have killed her.)*

3. Fern saw no difference in killing a little girl or a runt pig. She called this an injustice. Do you think this was an injustice (a wrong)? Why or why not?

4. Why do you think Mr. Arable finally gave Fern the runt pig?

5. Wilbur was an unusual pet—not like a cat, dog, or guinea pig. What are the advantages of having a pet like Wilbur? disadvantages?

**Prediction**
What will happen when Wilbur grows up?

**Drama Activity**
Role play Fern and her father's discussion. List reasons Mr. Arable would have for doing away with a runt pig. List Fern's reasons for keeping the pig. Pairs of students will role play, trying to persuade the other of his/her point of view.

**Art Activity**
Draw a picture of Wilbur, the perfect pig.

## Chapter II: "Wilbur" — Pages 8-12

**Vocabulary**
peered 9        enchanted 9        relieved 9        vanished 10
manure 12

**Vocabulary Activity**
Have students act out some of the words on the lists for Chapters 1 and 2 and see if classmates can guess the target words. For example, students might try to demonstrate "blissful," "peered," and "relieved" with facial expressions.

**Discussion Questions and Activities**
1. How did Fern treat Wilbur like a baby? *(page 8, put a bib on him, held him, fed him with a bottle)*

2. How was Wilbur different from a puppy? *(Page 9, "He crawled into the tunnel and disappeared from sight, completely covered with straw"; pages 10-11, "Wilbur amused himself in the mud along the edge of the brook…")*

3. How did Fern play with Wilbur? *(Page 10, She took him in the house and took him for walks in the doll carriage.)*

4. Why did Mr. Arable want to sell Wilbur? *(Page 12, Wilbur was eating too much food and all the other baby pigs had been sold.)*

5. Mother made a suggestion that made both Father and Fern happy. What was it? *(Page 12, Uncle Homer might buy Wilbur and Fern could visit him.)*

**Prediction**
Look at the title of the next chapter, "Escape." Who will escape? Why?

**Drama Activities**
1. With a classmate, act out the scene where Fern convinces Uncle Homer to buy Wilbur.

2. Monologue: Dramatize Fern telling Wilbur that he is moving to the Zuckermans'.

## Chapter III: "Escape" — Pages 13-24

**Vocabulary**

| perspiration 13 | patient 13 | grindstones 14 | scythes 14 |
| trough 16 | snout 18 | commotion 18 | asparagus 19 |
| pricked 19 | hullabaloo 22 | captivity 22 | appetizing 23 |
| slops 23 | | | |

**Vocabulary Activity**
Have students collaborate on making word maps for several words. An example:

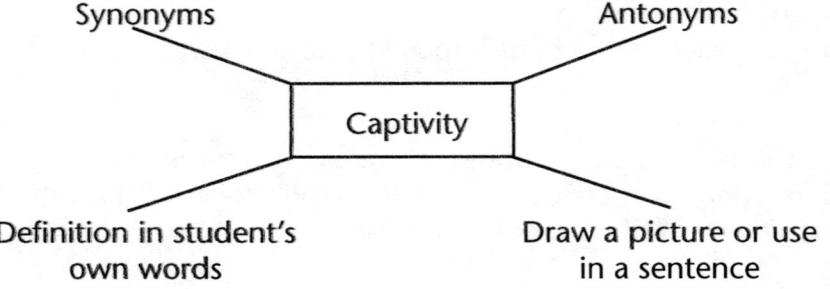

**Discussion Questions and Activities**

1. Why wasn't Wilbur happy in his new home? *(Page 16, He never had any fun—no walks, no rides, no swims.)*

2. The goose encouraged Wilbur to do bad things. Can you name some things Wilbur did? *(Pages 17-18, He pushed the board in the fence and went outside; went to the orchard; rooted up sod; rooted up the garden; and ran for the woods.)*

3. Compare Wilbur to the goose using a Venn diagram. How were they similar? How were they different?

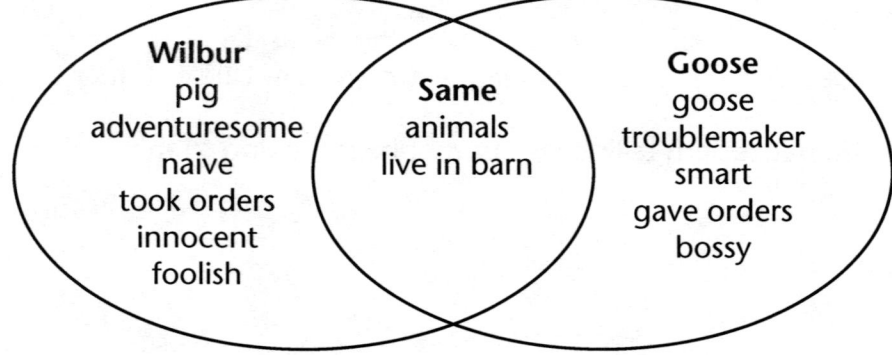

4. Wilbur didn't really like to be free. Prove this. *(Page 19, "If this is what it's like to be free, I believe I'd rather be penned up in my own yard.")*

5. Why was Wilbur displeased with freedom? *(Pages 18-23, He didn't know what to do, he didn't like all the excitement and noise, people screaming and trying to grab him, and he was frightened.)*

6. Have you ever wanted something and when you got it, you did not like it? Why? Teacher lists responses.

**Prediction**
The next chapter title is "Loneliness." Who will be lonely? Why?

**Writing Activity**
Write about something or sometime you got what you wanted but it was not what you expected.

**Game Idea**
Students make a game board by marking off a trail for Wilbur. The starting line might be the pigpen and the finish line would lead right back to the pigpen. Each square on the trail contains the name of a place or a character in the story or directions to "draw a card." Cards, which are made up by the students, instruct Wilbur to move ahead or move back a certain number of squares. For example: "Move ahead three spaces. Wilbur roots and digs in the orchard."

## Chapter IV: "Loneliness" — Pages 25-31

**Vocabulary**

| | | | |
|---|---|---|---|
| eaves 25 | occupation 26 | middlings 26 | hominy 26 |
| provender 26 | morsel 26 | goslings 28 | frolic 29 |
| glutton 29 | stealthily 30 | crafty 30 | dejected 30 |
| sulphur 31 | endure 31 | | |

**Vocabulary Activity**
Fill in the chart below with the proper words from the Synonym List.

| Vocabulary Word | Synonym | Synonym List |
|---|---|---|
| frolic | | dry food |
| provender | | secretively |
| morsel | | to romp |

endure                                    bite of food
crafty                                    put up with, tolerate
stealthily                                cunning, tricky

**Discussion Questions and Activities**
1. List Wilbur's planned time schedule. The teacher will write the list as the class tells the sequence. Verify by checking the book. *(pages 25-26)*

2. Why wasn't Wilbur happy? *(Page 27, He wanted a friend.)* Have you ever felt like this? What did you do about it?

3. Develop a class word association tree for the word "friend." (See Activity Sheet on page 17 of this guide.)

4. Why was Wilbur suddenly lonely? List in sequence the events that happened in this chapter. Did these events have anything to do with Wilbur's loneliness?

5. The lamb told Wilbur that "Pigs mean less than nothing to me." What do you think he meant? *(page 28)*

6. How did the rat Templeton say he spent his time? *(page 29, eating, gnawing, spying, and hiding)*

7. Begin an attribute web of things to remember about Templeton. (See pages 18-20 of this guide.)

8. Wilbur had to take some medicine. He said this was the worst day in his life. Have you ever had a day like this?

**Prediction**
Who do you think said to Wilbur, "I'll be a friend to you"? *(page 31)*

**Writing Activity**
The teacher will read *Alexander and the Terrible, Horrible, No Good, Very Bad Day* by Judith Viorst. The students may write about the worst day in their lives.

**Writing/Art Activity**
Write and illustrate your own *My Terrible Day Book*.

© Novel Units, Inc.                                              All rights reserved

## Activity Sheet

**Word Association Tree:** Let your mind imagine lots of words. The first word is given for you. Write two words the word FRIEND makes you think of. Follow the lines. Write whatever words you think of in the empty boxes.

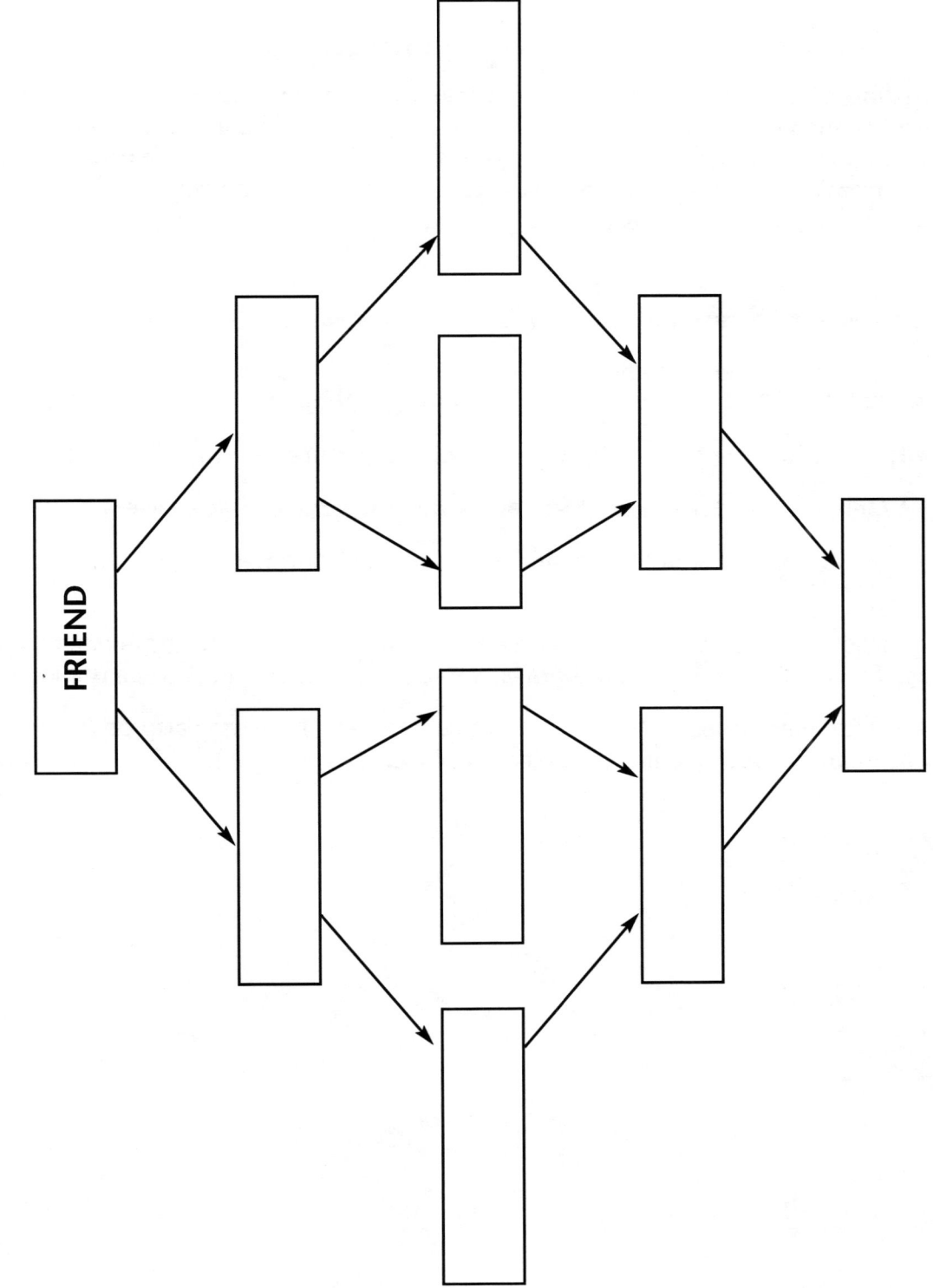

## Using Character Webs

Attribute Webs are simply a visual representation of a character from the novel. They provide a systematic way for the students to organize and recap the information they have about a particular character. Attribute webs may be used after reading the novel to recapitulate information about a particular character or completed gradually as information unfolds, done individually, or finished as a group project.

One type of character attribute web uses these divisions:

- How a character acts and feels. (How does the character feel in this picture? How would you feel if this happened to you? How do you think the character feels?)

- How a character looks. (Close your eyes and picture the character. Describe him to me.)

- Where a character lives. (Where and when does the character live?)

- How others feel about the character. (How does another specific character feel about our character?)

In group discussion about the student attribute webs and specific characters, the teacher can ask for **backup proof** from the novel. You can also include inferential thinking.

Attribute webs need not be confined to characters. They may also be used to organize information about a concept, object or place.

## Attribute Web

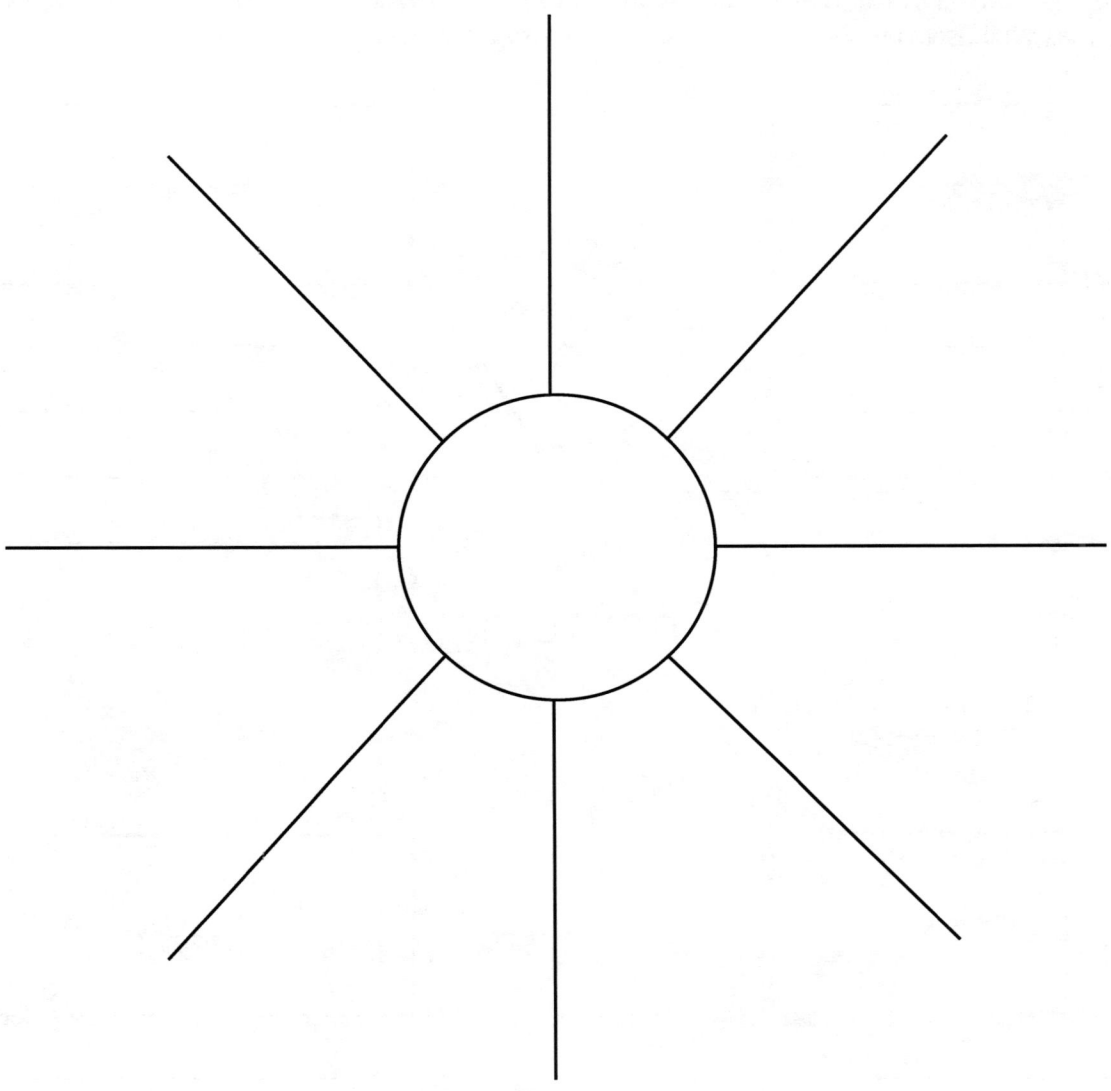

## Attribute Web

The attribute web below is designed to help you gather clues the author provides about what a character is like. Fill in the blanks with words and phrases which tell how the character acts and looks, as well as what the character says and what others say about him or her.

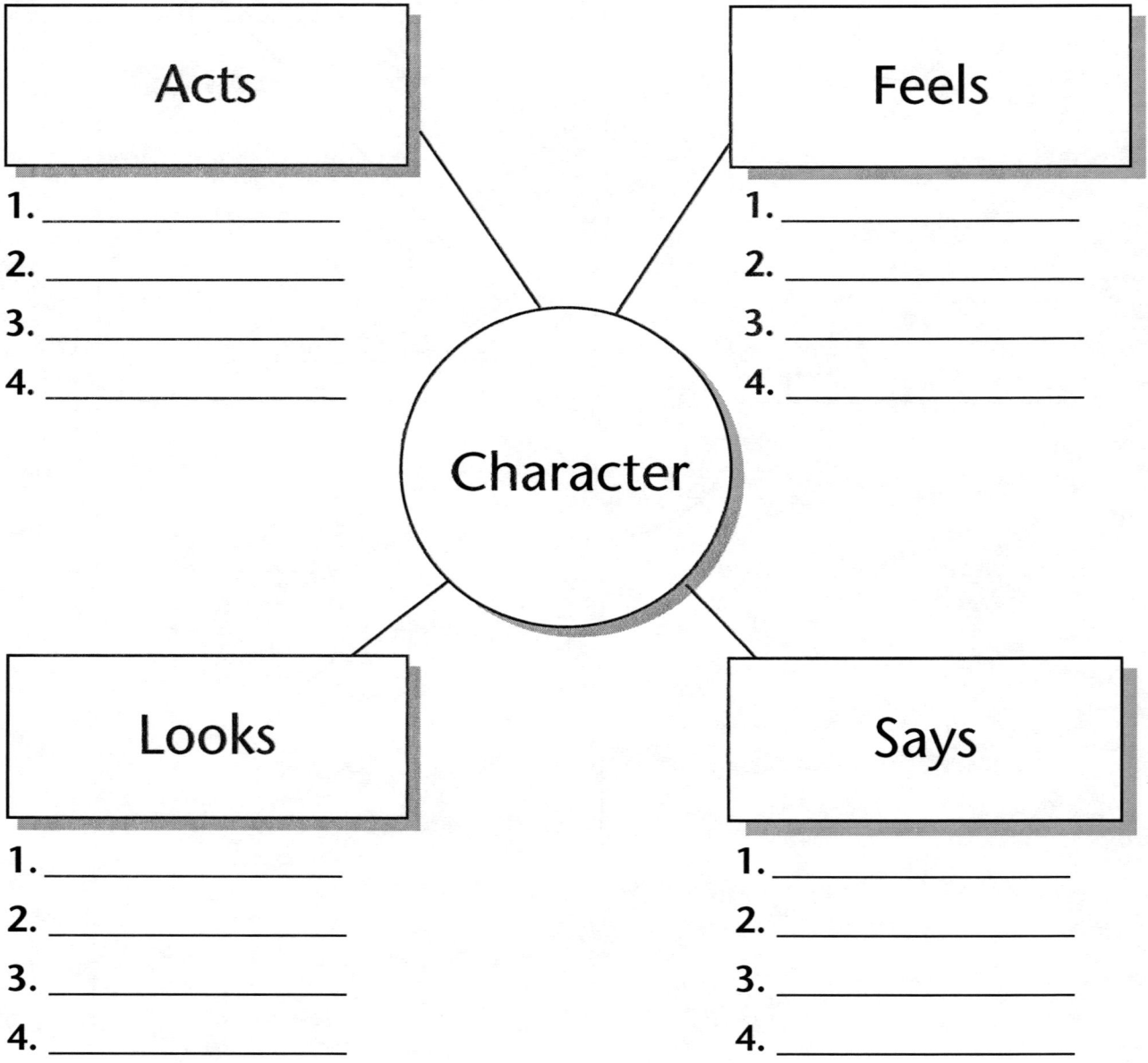

Acts
1. _____
2. _____
3. _____
4. _____

Feels
1. _____
2. _____
3. _____
4. _____

Looks
1. _____
2. _____
3. _____
4. _____

Says
1. _____
2. _____
3. _____
4. _____

© Novel Units, Inc.        All rights reserved

## Chapter V: "Charlotte" — Pages 32-41

**Vocabulary**

| | | | |
|---|---|---|---|
| clashers 32 | decent 32 | motionless 33 | appropriate 34 |
| disgust 34 | objectionable 35 | salutations 35 | blundered 37 |
| furiously 37 | horror 38 | detested 38 | midges 39 |
| miserable 39 | inheritance 39 | wits 40 | numerous 40 |
| innocent 40 | fierce 41 | brutal 41 | scheming 41 |

**Vocabulary Activity**
Complete the synonym chains.

decent - respectable - adequate - satisfactory - passable -
appropriate - suitable - proper - fitting -
blunder - mistake - error -
furious - angry - raging -
detest - hate - despise -
wits - wisdom - mind - sense - understanding -

**Discussion Questions and Activities**

1. How did Wilbur find his mysterious friend? *(Page 34, He called out, "Will the party who addressed me at bedtime last night kindly make himself or herself known by giving an appropriate sign or signal!")*

2. Wilbur was shocked and disgusted with Charlotte's eating habits. Make a T-comparison of what Charlotte and Wilbur ate. Would you rather share a meal with Charlotte or Wilbur?

| Charlotte | Wilbur |
|---|---|
| *crickets, flies, bugs, grasshoppers, centipedes, beetles, gnats, mosquitoes, cockroaches, midges* | *milk, crusts, potato skins, doughnuts, custard* |

3. What did Charlotte learn from her family? *(page 39, trapper's instinct—how to find things to eat and stay alive)*

4. Why did Charlotte say it was good that spiders eat bugs? *(Page 40, "...if I didn't catch bugs and eat them, bugs would increase and multiply and get so numerous that they'd destroy the earth...")*

© Novel Units, Inc.            All rights reserved

5. Why did the goose say Wilbur was an innocent little pig? *(page 40, because Wilbur didn't know that Mr. Zuckerman and Lurvy were plotting to kill him)*

6. Wilbur said friendship is a gamble because there are bad characteristics, as well as good characteristics, in every individual. List all of Charlotte's good points, as well as her bad points, on a T-diagram.

**Charlotte**

| Good | Bad |
|---|---|
| affectionate | bloodthirsty |
| loyal | brutal |
| pretty | scheming |
| clever | fierce |
| kind | bold |
| true | cruel |
| skillful | |

7. Begin an attribute web for Charlotte and Wilbur.

**Prediction**
What do you think Templeton will do with the egg? What do you think will happen to the egg?

**Writing Activity**
Write a letter to Wilbur giving him some advice about making friends, accepting friends as they are, and getting along with friends.

**Art Activities**
1. Make a spider web design using yarn or string.

2. Create a shoebox diagram of the barn.

**Research Activity**
Complete the Farm Animal Chart on the following page.

# Farm Animal Chart

| | | | | | | |
|---|---|---|---|---|---|---|
| **Male:** | horse | bull | sheep | gander | rooster | goat |
| **Female:** | mare | cow | ewe | goose | hen | goat |
| **Offspring:** | colt | calf | lamb | gosling | chick | kid |

Students should be familiar with the names of common barn yard animals and the varying names within animal families. The teacher will write part of the above information on the board and the class will help complete the chart.

The farm yard animals play an important role in *Charlotte's Web*. The life cycles of Wilbur and Charlotte are important in the book. Divide the class into small groups. Use the materials at the library table to complete the chart below on each of the animals—food, habitat, enemies, etc.

| | Spider | Bull | Sheep | Gander | Pig | Goat |
|---|---|---|---|---|---|---|
| **Number of Siblings** | | | | | | |
| **Weight at Birth** | | | | | | |
| **Food** | | | | | | |
| **Enemies** | | | | | | |
| **Habitat** | | | | | | |
| **Lifetime** | | | | | | |

© Novel Units, Inc.　　　　　　　　　　　　　　　　　　　　　　All rights reserved

## Chapter VI: "Summer Days" — Pages 42-47

**Vocabulary**

| phoebe 43 | interlude 43 | desperately 44 | gratified 44 |
| unremitting 44 | morals 46 | conscience 46 | decency 46 |
| rodent 46 | compunctions 46 | untenable 4 | lair 47 |

**Vocabulary Activity**
Complete each of the following sentences. Your completed sentences should make sense and show that you understand what the underlined word means.

1. The dog hunted <u>desperately</u> for _____.
2. The <u>gratified</u> teacher _____.
3. The coach demanded <u>unremitting</u> effort from _____.
4. The <u>lair</u> is located _____.
5. The boy's <u>conscience</u> _____.
6. <u>Compunction</u> is necessary for _____.

**Discussion Questions and Activities**
1. Why did the goose and gander and all the animals worry about Templeton? Make an attribute web with all the words that describe Templeton.

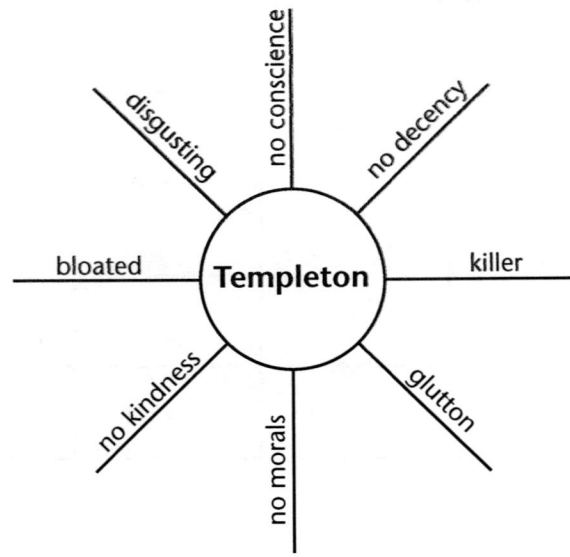

© Novel Units, Inc.                                                All rights reserved

2. Would you trust Templeton? Why or why not?

3. Compare Charlotte and Templeton using a T-diagram.

| Charlotte | Templeton |
|---|---|
| *Killer* | *Killer* |
| *Scheming* | *No conscience* |
| *Kind* | *No kindness* |
| *Skillful* | *No decency* |

4. The gander made a deal with Templeton. What was it? *(Page 45, He could have the dud egg that didn't hatch but he must not touch the goslings.)*

5. Do you think you could make a deal with a character like Templeton? Why or why not?

**Prediction**
How will the dud egg be important?

**Writing Activity**
The author describes life in the barn with Wilbur. Reread the description and notice how the author makes the reader see, feel, smell, and hear what Wilbur did. Then describe some place you have been. Include as many details as you can that describe what you saw, felt, smelled, heard, and tasted.

## Chapter VII: "Bad News" — Pages 48-51

**Vocabulary**
    loathed 48    anaesthetic 48    rigid 49    conspiracy 49
    hysterics 51

**Vocabulary Activity**
Complete the synonym chains.

    loathe - hate - detest -
    anaesthetic - drug -
    rigid - stiff - rigorous - inflexible - strict -
    conspiracy - plot - intrigue -
    hysterics - frenzy -

**Discussion Questions and Activities**
1. What bad news did the sheep give Wilbur? *(Page 49, There's was a plot to kill Wilbur.)*

2. How could Wilbur be sure the sheep was telling the truth? Prove it. *(Page 49, "I'm an old sheep and I see the same thing, same old business, year after year. Arable arrives with his .22, shoots the ...")*

3. Compare Charlotte to the sheep using a Venn diagram. How were they similar and how were they different?

4. Charlotte said she will save Wilbur's life. How do you think a little spider could save a pig's life?

5. What would you do to save Wilbur's life?

6. What was Wilbur's reaction to the sheep's news? *(Page 50, Wilbur cried and carried on in a childish way.)*

7. How did you feel when the sheep said Wilbur was going to be killed?

**Prediction**
How can Charlotte save Wilbur?

**Writing Activity**
Suppose you are Wilbur. What would you write in your diary on this sad day? Write a short entry and share with a classmate.

## Chapter VIII: "A Talk At Home" — Pages 52-54

**Vocabulary:**
vaguely 53    gratified 53    unremitting 53    rambled 54

**Vocabulary Activity:**
Choose the word in each list below which does NOT belong with the others and be prepared to explain why.

**vaguely, uncertainly, specifically, indefinitely**

*(Specifically shows explicit detail; the other words suggest a lack of clarity, a shadowy haziness.)*

### gratified, displeased, satisfied, pleased
(*Displeased* shows unhappiness; the other words express pleasure or contentment.)

### unremitting, pardon, incessant, retain
(*Pardon* shows a change in position; the other words suggest not relaxing or stopping.)

### ramble, stroll, wander, stride, saunter
(*Stride* means walk with a purpose; the other words suggest movement or travel without a destination or purpose.)

**Discussion Questions and Activities**

1. Fern told her parents what the animals in the barn were talking about. This upset her mother. What would your mother do if you told her about talking animals? Do you believe that animals talk? communicate? What is the difference between talking and communicating? Make a word definition chart with the class.

| Talk | Communicate |
|---|---|
| • To speak | • To make known |
| • Communicate with spoken language | • Share feelings, thoughts |
| • Use words that can be written as well as spoken | • Exchange of thoughts and messages |
| | • Signals |
| | • Sign language |
| | • Body language |

2. Charlotte used lots of big words but we can understand what she meant because she explained. What did she mean when she said, "...every one of us ... will be gratified to learn that after four weeks of unremitting effort and patience on the part of the goose, she now has something to show for it"? *(page 53-54)*

3. Why didn't Mr. Arable worry about Fern? *(Page 54, "She's just got a lively imagination.")* Do your fathers worry about all the things mothers worry about? Why do you suppose this is so?

**Writing Activity**

Mrs. Arable mentions talking to the doctor about Fern. Perhaps she will also write to Dear Abby for advice. Write a letter for her to Dear Abby and a response to the worried mother.

## Chapter IX: "Wilbur's Boast" — Pages 55-65

**Vocabulary**
  witnessed 55    spinnerets 56    oblige 57    summoning 58
  sedentary 60    troupe 63

**Vocabulary Activity**
Develop word maps for several vocabulary words. Display as part of the bulletin board.

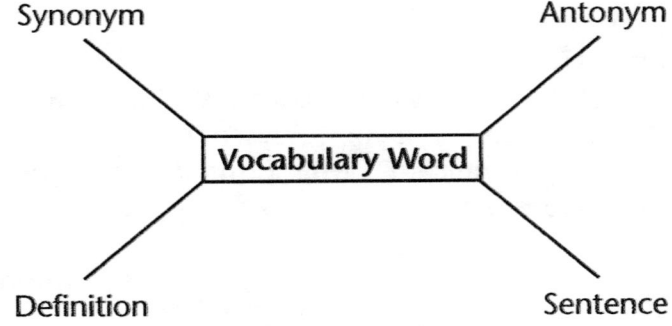

**Discussion Questions and Activities**
1. Why did Charlotte say her legs had seven sections? *(Page 55, Her legs had to be very special to make webs.)*

2. Why was Wilbur unable to spin a web? *(Page 58, He lacked a set of spinnerets and knowledge.)*

3. Why was this chapter funny?

**Prediction**
The next chapter is entitled "An Explosion." What might happen? Who will be involved?

**Research Activity**
Find out all you can about spiders (appearance, habits, food, number of siblings, etc.). Write a short report and present it to your group.

## Chapter X: "An Explosion"— Pages 66-76

**Vocabulary**
  gullible 67    crisis 68    straddled 69    scuttled 72
  surly 74       astride 75   bestirred 75    drowsed 75

© Novel Units, Inc.

**Vocabulary Activity**
Complete each of the following sentences. Your completed sentences should make sense and show that you know that you understand what the underlined word means.

1. The gullible man _____.
2. The army responded to the crisis by _____.
3. The child straddled the pony and _____.
4. The sailors scuttled _____.
5. The bear became surly when _____.
6. Astride the horse _____.
7. Dad drowsed in _____.

**Discussion Questions and Activities**
1. How did Charlotte propose to save Wilbur's life? *(page 67, play a trick on Zuckerman)*

2. How would you explain what Charlotte thought, "I can surely fool a man. People are not as smart as bugs"? *(page 67)*

3. What caused the explosion in the barn? *(Page 72, Avery was teasing Fern and he tried to knock down Charlotte and her web. He fell on Wilbur's trough and broke the rotten egg.)*

4. How did the unhatched goose egg save Charlotte? *(Pages 72-73, The smell was so bad that Avery and Fern left the barn and forgot about Charlotte and her web.)*

5. Compare Avery and Fern using a Venn Diagram. How were they alike and how were they different? Did their parents treat them differently? Why?

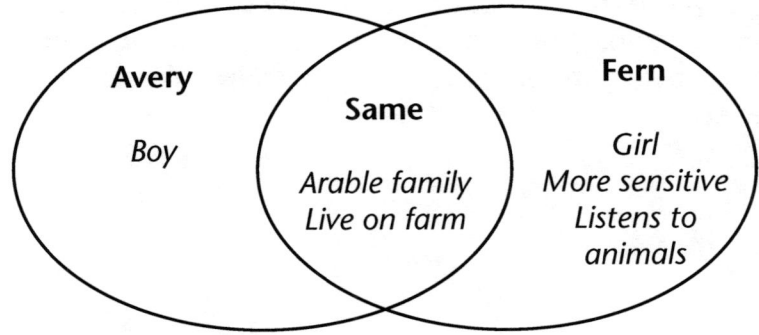

**Prediction**
Do you really think Charlotte will be able to save Wilbur? Why or why not?

**Writing Activities**
1. Make up a "graffiti board" of words to describe characters. (Names of characters are evenly spaced on a large piece of paper. Students write descriptions in various letterings and positions near the appropriate name.)

2. Write an entry in Wilbur's diary.

3. Change three things in this chapter and explain how the changes would make a difference in the outcome of the chapter.

**Art Activities**
1. Mural (bulletin board idea): With a group of students, create a mural showing the barn. Then paint, cut out, and mount the story's characters on the mural.

2. Design a mobile of important characters and objects from the story.

3. Create a pig and spider exhibit with classmates. This will include art, research reports, stories, and poems.

4. Collect a spider's web. To collect webs, you will need sturdy black or colored paper. Flocked paper, which has a rough surface, is best. A can of white spray paint and one of clear lacquer are also needed.

   To collect the web, first scare off the spider so it will not be hurt by the paint and will be able to go make a new web. Hold the spray can about two feet from the web and spray evenly. Let the coat dry and spray again, laying on several coats to strengthen the web before cutting it. While the last coat is still slightly damp, bring a piece of paper carefully behind and press it against the web so it catches. Carefully cut any support threads which extend beyond the paper. After you have successfully collected the web on paper, spray it with a layer of clear lacquer for protection.

## Chapter XI: "The Miracle" — Pages 77-85

**Vocabulary**

| delicate 77 | exertions 79 | solemnly 79 | bewilderment 80 |
| wondrous 83 | attraction 85 | | |

**Vocabulary Activity**
Combine two vocabulary words into a meaningful sentence.

**Discussion Questions and Activities**

1. Brainstorm the meanings of the word *miracle*:

   — an event that can't be explained by laws of nature

   — a person, thing, or event that excites people

2. When did Charlotte think about her plan to save Wilbur? *(Page 63, "When I'm hanging head-down at the top of my web. That's when I do my thinking, because then all the blood is in my head.")*

3. When and where do you do your best thinking?

4. How was Charlotte's trick going to save Wilbur?

5. How did the miracle spider web change life for Wilbur and the Zuckermans? Complete the Cause-Effect Chart with the class.

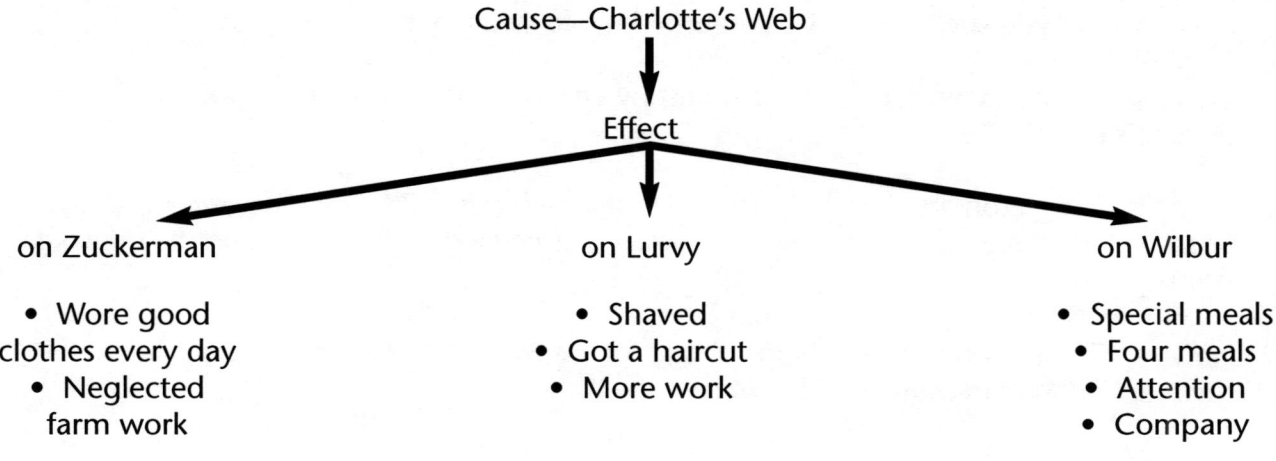

**Prediction**
How will Charlotte's message in the web bring more changes?

## Chapter XII: "A Meeting" — Pages 86-91

**Vocabulary**

| | | | |
|---|---|---|---|
| idiosyncrasy 86 | proceed 87 | impress 89 | particle 89 |
| access 89 | baser 90 | instincts 90 | destiny 90 |
| quivered 91 | adjourned 91 | sensational 91 | |

**Vocabulary Activity**
Match each of the vocabulary words above with its synonym from the synonym list.

| Answer | Synonym |
|---|---|
| idiosyncrasy | quirk |
| proceed | go on |
| impress | influence |
| particle | small piece |
| access | path or opportunity to come near |
| destiny | fate or fortune |
| quivered | shake |
| adjourned | suspend, postpone |
| sensational | thrilling |

**Discussion Questions and Activities**

1. Charlotte called a meeting of the barn animals to suggest new ideas for the web. What words would you use to describe Wilbur? Why do you make this suggestion?

2. On page 90 the sheep said, "Wilbur's destiny and your destiny are closely linked." What does this mean?

3. Why did Templeton agree to help save Wilbur's life? *(Page 90, The sheep appealed to his baser instincts. If Wilbur was killed, there would not be food in the trough and the rat would be hungry.)*

4. How was Templeton going to help? *(Page 89, He would tear out advertisements and bring them to Charlotte to copy for words to describe Wilbur.)*

**Prediction**
What reaction will there be for the "terrific" sign?

**Writing and Art Activities**
1. Make a collection of words from magazines to describe one of the other animals, besides Wilbur, in *Charlotte's Web*. Draw a picture of the animal. Glue the magazine words around the animal.

2. Write and draw an advertisement for Wilbur.

3. Create a slogan for Wilbur.

## Chapter XIII: "Good Progress" — Pages 92-104

**Vocabulary**
| | | | |
|---|---|---|---|
| orb 92 | foundation 93 | descend 94 | admiration 96 |
| wondrous 96 | alders 97 | astonishing 97 | discarded 97 |
| tattered 97 | rummaging 97 | triumphantly 99 | mercilessly 103 |
| lashed 103 | aeronaut 103 | dung 104 | |

**Vocabulary Activity**
Good readers make good guesses. Classify the vocabulary words: names of things (nouns); action words (verbs); and describing words (adjectives and adverbs). Work in groups to sort the words. Check words in the dictionary. (We have classified the words as they are used in the book. Some of the words could be classified in more than one category.)

Nouns: orb - foundation - admiration - alders - aeronaut - dung
Verbs: descend - rummaging - lashed
Describing Words: mercilessly - wondrous - astonishing - discarded - tattered - triumphantly

**Discussion Questions and Activities**
1. What were the descriptive words suggested by Templeton? *(pages 98-99, crunchy, preshrunk, radiant)* What was wrong with some of these words?

2. What did the chapter title, "Good Progress" mean? *(Charlotte was making progress in her attempt to save Wilbur.)*

3. What did Lurvy have to do to change Wilbur's pigpen? *(page 96, no more cow manure thrown into the pigpen, new clean straw for bedding every day)*

**Research Activity**
Observe a spider web. Where do you think the spider started the web? Make a diagram of the spider web. Did the spider abandon the web?

## Chapter XIV: "Dr. Dorian" — Pages 105-112

fascinating 105   aloft 106      sociable 107   enchanting 107
miraculous 109    fidgeted 110   civilly 110    incessant 110

**Vocabulary Activity**
Use the vocabulary words in sentences. How many words can you combine in a meaningful sentence?

**Discussion Questions and Activities**
1. Was Dr. Dorian a wise man? Why or why not?

2. How is he like your family doctor?

3. Dr. Dorian pointed out that the web itself was a miracle. How do you think the spider learned to spin webs?

4. What things do animals do instinctively? What things might be learned?

5. What is "normal" for an eight-year-old girl? for a boy?

**Drama Activity**
Role play Mrs. Arable telling Fern's father about the trip to the doctor. What questions might he ask?

## Chapter XV: "The Crickets" — Pages 113-117

**Vocabulary**

monotonous 113   anxiety 114    radiant 114    befriended 114
reputation 114   mere 115       confident 115  distinguish 115
inconvenient 116 amazement 116  versatile 116

**Vocabulary Activity**
Make a crossword puzzle on graph paper using at least five words. Write the clues and work out the answers. Exchange puzzles with a classmate.

**Discussion Questions and Activities**
1. What's the real purpose of this chapter, "The Crickets"? *(Pages 113-117, Time was passing quickly for Charlotte and Wilbur. The author tells us that both Charlotte and Wilbur had worries about time passing.)*

2. What was Wilbur worried about? *(Page 115, "If he could distinguish himself at the Fair and maybe win some prize money, he was sure Zuckerman would let him live.")*

3. What was Charlotte worried about? *(page 117, her family duties of building a little egg sac and laying her eggs)*

4. Why couldn't Charlotte go to the Fair with Wilbur? *(Page 117, She had to lay eggs.)*

**Prediction**
How will Charlotte arrange to go to the Fair?

**Research Activity**
How many eggs does a spider lay?

**Writing Activity**
What would Wilbur write in these lazy days of summer before the Fair? Write a diary entry.

## Chapter XVI: "Off to the Fair" — Pages 118-129

**Vocabulary**

| | | | |
|---|---|---|---|
| cautiously 121 | trickling 121 | delicious 121 | discarded 123 |
| foul 123 | particles 123 | veritable 123 | gnawed 123 |
| appetizing 123 | surpass 123 | resist 124 | bewitched 125 |
| pummel 125 | lacerated 125 | | |

**Vocabulary Activity**
Students will make predictions about how the author will use the vocabulary: setting, characters, problem, action.

**Discussion Questions and Activities**
1. How did the family prepare to go to the Fair?

2. On pages 122-123, the old sheep gave Templeton reasons why he should go to the Fair. Why was this funny?

3. Why did Charlotte and Templeton decide to go to the Fair? *(Page 122, Wilbur might need help.)*

4. Explain why Wilbur fainted in the story. *(pages 127, 159)*

**Prediction**
Will Wilbur need Charlotte's and Templeton's help at the Fair? Are Templeton's motives for going to the Fair different from Charlotte's?

## Chapter XVII: "Uncle" — Pages 130-137
**Vocabulary**
blatting 130    enormous 130    cautioned 131    unattractive 135

**Vocabulary Activity**
Take the vocabulary words for several chapters. Play a 20 questions type game (pairs, groups, or whole class). One student, or the teacher, selects a word for the class or group to identify by asking up to 20 questions (or 10 questions) about the word which may be answered by "yes," "no," or "sometimes."

**Discussion Questions and Activities**
1. Charlotte was not herself. Find some clues as to what may be wrong. *(page 136, no energy, looked swollen, seemed listless)*

2. What advantages did Uncle have over Wilbur at the Fair? *(page 134, his size and weight)*

3. On what criteria do you think a pig was judged at the Fair?

**Prediction**
What will happen if Wilbur wins at the Fair? What could happen if he loses?

## Chapter XVIII: "The Cool of the Evening" — Pages 138-143
**Vocabulary**
keen 138         detected 138     humble 140       sneered 140
fetching 140     paradise 140     schemer 140      masterpiece 143

**Vocabulary Activity**
Each student or cooperative group will make a poster, banner, or sign to advertise their word or words. The ad must show what the word means and how to pronounce it. The words will be displayed and should be signed by the artist(s).

**Discussion Questions and Activities**
1. On page 140 Charlotte said, "It is the last word I shall ever write." What do you think is going to happen?

2. Templeton brought the word *humble* for Charlotte to write above Wilbur's pen. Was this a good word to describe Wilbur? Why or why not?

3. One page 143, Charlotte said she was making something for herself—a masterpiece. What do you think it will be? What is a *masterpiece*?

4. Why did Fern have the best time ever at the Fair? *(Page 139, Fern met Henry Fussy and rode on the Ferris wheel.)*

5. How had Fern changed in the story? *(Page 139, Fern spent less time with Wilbur and more time with Henry.)*

**Prediction**
Will Wilbur's personality change if he wins or if he loses at the fair?

# Chapter XIX: "The Egg Sac" — Pages 144-154
**Vocabulary**

| | | | |
|---|---|---|---|
| magnum opus 144 | languishing 146 | carousing 148 | gorge 148 |
| acute 148 | indigestion 148 | licked 148 | hankering 148 |
| bloated 148 | suspiciously 149 | enormous 150 | crouched 153 |

**Vocabulary Activity**
List the vocabulary words for the day on large sheets of paper. Leave space for students to a) illustrate the meaning next to each word; b) list a memory device to remember the word; c) write the dictionary symbols to show how the word is pronounced.

**Discussion Questions and Activities**
1. Let's add some descriptive words to Templeton's attribute web. *(disgusting, glutton, bloated, dopey, mean)*

2. Charlotte had two jobs to do at the Fair. What were they? *(page 153, to lay her eggs and to save Wilbur's life)*

3. Was the information about spider eggs accurate? What kind of spider was Charlotte? *(page 37, Cavatica)* What will happen to Charlotte?

**Prediction**
What will the special award be? The next chapter is "The Hour of Triumph." What does to word "triumph" have to do with Wilbur and Charlotte?

## Chapter XX: "The Hour of Triumph" — Pages 155-162
**Vocabulary**
extraordinary 155   unique 157         sundry 157         phenomenon 157
analysis 157        supernatural 157   magnificent 158    assured 158
revived 159         meekly 161

**Vocabulary Activity**
Use a "Trivial Pursuit" board with vocabulary words and definitions on 3 x 5 cards for each category. Players must give the word for the definition which is read aloud to score.

**Discussion Questions and Activities**
1. Why was Wilbur given a special prize at the Fair? *(Pages 157-158, Because of the phenomenon of words written about him on a cobweb.)*

2. How did Wilbur react to the prize? *(Page 159, He fainted.)* How did Mr. Zuckerman react? Avery? Make a Cause-Effect Chart.

3. How did Templeton save the day and the prize for Wilbur? *(Page 159, When Wilbur fainted and passed out, Templeton revived him by biting his tail.)*

**Prediction**
How is this story going to end? In this story Wilbur had problems. What is the resolution of the problems?

**Writing Activity**
What would Fern write in her diary? How would her diary entry differ from Avery's or her father's? Choose one of the characters and write the important events of the day at the Fair as they saw it.

© Novel Units, Inc.                                                                              All rights reserved

## Chapter XXI: "Last Day" — Pages 163-171

**Vocabulary**

| assured 163 | secure 163 | sentiments 165 | desolation 165 |
| ridiculous 165 | dazed 166 | relaxation 168 | mimicked 168 |
| desperate 168 | | | |

**Vocabulary Activity**
Make a vocabulary activity for a classmate. Use more than the vocabulary from just this chapter. Pick five words and write synonyms. Arrange the words and synonyms so they may be matched. Write an answer key.

**Discussion Questions and Activities**
1. How did Templeton help in the story? *(got magazine clippings at the dump and a piece of string for Charlotte to spin a web; saved Charlotte's life with the rotten goose egg; bit Wilbur's tail and brought him out of the faint; got Charlotte's egg sac)*

2. Why did Wilbur get Templeton to take down Charlotte's egg sac? *(pages 166-167, so that Charlotte's 514 baby spiders would hatch in the barn)*

3. Why did Wilbur wink at Charlotte? *(page 171, to say goodbye and because he held her egg sac in his mouth so he could not talk)*

**Writing Activity**
No one was with Charlotte when she died. There was no grave or burial ceremony in her honor. Write what could have been said about her character and her actions.

## Chapter XXII: "A Warm Wind" — Pages 172-184

**Vocabulary**

| affectionate 173 | retorted 173 | lee 174 | gigantic 175 |
| frantic 179 | tranquil 183 | garrulous 183 | |

**Discussion Questions and Activities**
1. Complete the attribute webs for Wilbur, Templeton, and Charlotte.

**Vocabulary Activity**
Put the vocabulary words in alphabetical order. Define each word. Use each word in a sentence.

## Post-reading Questions

1. What did Wilbur learn?

2. How was the setting important?

3. Did any of the characters act in ways that were surprising?

4. What do you know about Wilbur that the Zuckermans did not know?

5. Was there a "bad guy" in this story? Who? How would the story have been different without him?

6. Where do you suppose the author got his ideas for this story?

7. What other stories does this remind you of?

8. Find some words or phrases in the story which are unusual.

9. Which parts of the story do you think were funny?

10. Discuss the differences between realism and fantasy using a T-chart. Help students see that *Charlotte's Web* contains elements of both realism and fantasy by having them categorize the setting, characters, actions, and problems in the story as realistic or fantastic. A sample T-chart is shown below.

| Realism | Fantasy |
| --- | --- |
| Setting—our world | Setting—often combines real world and make-believe |
| Characters—like us | Characters—often combines true-to-life characters with unusual ones like talking animals or tiny people |
| Action—could happen but is not a true story | Action—some of the story could never happen |
| Problem—could be ours | Problem—some problems are true-to-life, but most are very unusual |

# Culminating Activities

**Drama Activities**
1. Choose your favorite part of the story, and stage a "Reader's Theater" production with classmates. (You will need to rewrite the section so that one person reads the part of the narrator, and the characters' parts are split up among the remaining readers.) Sit in a semi-circle so that you can see each other's expressions as you read. Use simple props to identify the characters.

2. Retell the story to a friend. You might use puppets, or even make your own finger puppets to liven up the story.

**Point of View**
Divide the class into small groups. Each person in a group should tell the story from a different point of view. Encourage the students to imitate the characters they choose with voice and gestures.

**Vocabulary Game**
The students will choose vocabulary words to be used in Bingo. They will make a set of varied Bingo cards with printed words and a matching set of words with definitions for a caller. The caller reads the definition. All who have found the answer, mark it on the card until a winner is found.

## Teacher Facts About Spiders

| | |
|---|---|
| Class: | Arachnida (spiders, scorpions, ticks, and mites) |
| Order: | Araneae (spiders) |
| Family: | There are 23 families of spiders in North America. |
| Habitat: | Varies with the species. |
| Senses: | Spiders have eight eyes arranged or grouped by characterized species. Spiders that trap are extremely short-sighted. Only spiders that hunt have good eyesight. Orb weavers, like Charlotte, locate prey by feeling the vibration and tension of the threads in the web, then quickly turn the captive with their legs while their fourth legs pull out silk and wrap the victim. The prey is bitten before being carried to the center of the web or to the spider's retreat in the corner. |

Enemies: Include other spiders and some kinds of insects and birds. These enemies help to control the spider populations, which are affected also by parasites and availability of food.

Body: Spiders have two body parts: a cephalothorax, covered by a shield, and an abdomen. Four pairs of legs are attached to the cephalothorax. The legs end in either two or three claws. Nearly all spiders have eight simple eyes.

The cephalothorax (combined head and thorax) contains the brain, poison glands, and stomach. In the abdomen are the heart, digestive tract, reproductive organs, lungs, respiratory trachea and silk glands. The two parts are connected by a <u>thin</u> stalk through which pass the aorta, intestine, nerve cord, and some muscles.

Spider jaws in the front of the head are tipped by fangs with a duct from a poison gland.

Food: Spiders feed on living prey which may be killed or paralyzed with poison. Juices from the digestive glands liquefy the prey before it is sucked into the mouth. Spiders with few teeth on their jaws may suck out the insides of the prey and discard the empty shell.

Family Life: Female spiders weave silk baskets or egg sacs to cradle jelly-like eggs. Some species make several egg sacs, each containing several hundred eggs. Species that take care of their young usually produce fewer eggs. Weeks later, or sometimes not until the following spring, the young spiderlings emerge.

Unusual Facts: Growth of a spider requires shedding its exoskeleton 4 to 12 times before maturity. In the process of shedding, a previously lost leg may be replaced by a new leg. Most spiders live one or two seasons. The silk produced by spiders is used in many ways. Most spiders make silken egg cases. Some species use silk to make a nursery for spiderlings. Many hide in silk tunnels or line their burrows with silk. Prey may be caught in webs or snares. Spiderlings use silk for <u>ballooning</u> to move to a new area.

# Using the *Charlotte's Web* Poster

**Prereading Discussion**
1. Describe the figures in the poster. What sorts of animals are they?
2. Can you make any predictions about the story?
3. What kind of story do you expect—biography, mythical tale, adventure, or science fiction? Give reasons to support or reject each type of story.

**Post-reading Discussion**
1. Why is this an appropriate/inappropriate poster for the book?
2. Which characters from the book can you recognize in the poster? Why?
3. Does the poster reveal anything about the setting of the novel (place and time)?
4. Why is the poster a good summary of the book?
5. What is the most prominent object in the poster? Why is this appropriate?
6. Look for passages in the book which particularly suggest the illustration in the poster.

**Art of the Poster**
1. Describe the poster relative to:

   color          line          shape          space          texture

2. Compare the poster to other posters and illustrations, filling in a comparison chart:

| Novel Title | Color | Line | Shape | Space | Texture |
|---|---|---|---|---|---|
|  |  |  |  |  |  |
|  |  |  |  |  |  |
|  |  |  |  |  |  |
|  |  |  |  |  |  |
|  |  |  |  |  |  |

3. Add color to black and white illustrations.

**Writing Prompts**
1. Why did the illustrator choose a particular medium?
2. Which is more important to a book—the author or illustrator? Why? What does each add to a book's impact?
3. "A picture is worth a thousand words." Support or deny.

# Assessment for *Charlotte's Web*

Assessment is an ongoing process, more than a quiz at the end of the book. Points may be added to show the level of achievement. When an item is completed, the teacher and the student check it.

Name _____  Date _____

**Student**     **Teacher**

_____     _____     1. Make a character web of a character in *Charlotte's Web*. (See pages 18-20 of this guide.)

_____     _____     2. Select your best writing project and polish it to share with classmates.

_____     _____     3. Compare Charlotte and Templeton using a T-diagram.

_____     _____     4. Research spiders and write a short report.

_____     _____     5. Design a spider web using yarn or string.

_____     _____     6. Complete the Farm Animal Chart on page 23 of this guide.

_____     _____     7. Change three things in this novel and explain to a classmate how the changes would make a difference.

_____     _____     8. Make a mobile of important characters and objects in the story.

_____     _____     9. Write a ten question quiz for a classmate. Make an answer sheet.

_____     _____     10. Participate in a dramatic activity.

Comments: